NEPTUNE

NEPTUNE

SEYMOUR SIMON

MORROW JUNIOR BOOKS
New York

PHOTO AND ART CREDITS
All photographs courtesy of Jet Propulsion Laboratory/NASA.
Artwork on pages 8, 9, and 10 by Ann Neumann.

The text type is 18 pt. ITC Garamond Book.

Copyright © 1991 by Seymour Simon

Printed in Singapore at Tien Wah Press.

1   2   3   4   5   6   7   8   9   10

Library of Congress Cataloging-in-Publication Data
Simon, Seymour.
Neptune / Seymour Simon.
p.   cm.
Summary: Discusses the physical features and moons of the planet
Neptune and how we have gained our knowledge of this giant world.
ISBN 0-688-09631-X (trade).—ISBN 0-688-09632-8 (library)
1. Neptune (Planet)—Juvenile literature.   [1. Neptune (Planet)]
I. Title.
QB691.S56   1991
523.4'81—dc20   90-13213   CIP   AC

To the *Voyager* scientists, engineers,
and technicians who provided us
with these wonderful photographs
of Neptune

Neptune cannot be seen from Earth by the unaided eye. Even when viewed through a telescope, it looks like a tiny blue dot as distant as the stars. In fact, Galileo saw Neptune through his small telescope almost four hundred years ago, but mistook it for a star. Neptune was first identified as a planet in 1846 at the Berlin Observatory in Germany. Later, the planet was named Neptune after the Roman god of the sea.

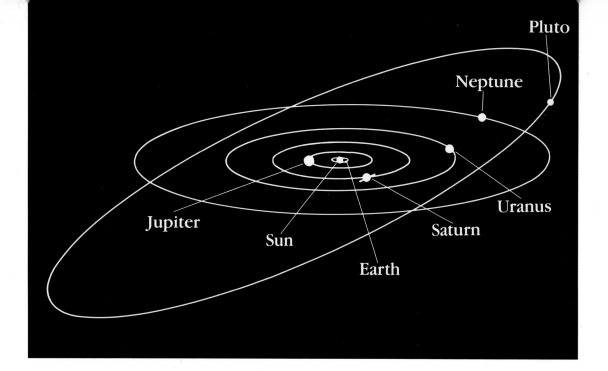

Neptune is the eighth planet in the Solar System and takes 165 years to orbit the sun. Pluto is the ninth planet and takes almost 250 years to circle the sun. But Pluto has an odd orbit that brings it closer to the sun than Neptune for 20 out of every 250 years. So between 1979 and 1999, Neptune is the outermost of the planets.

Neptune is about 2.8 billion miles from the sun, thirty times farther away than planet Earth. Like Jupiter, Saturn, and Uranus, Neptune is a giant planet made up mostly of gases. Neptune is about thirty thousand miles across, just a bit smaller than Uranus. If Neptune were hollow, about forty-two Earths could fit inside.

The *Voyager 2* spacecraft, seen in the painting on the right, was launched from Earth on August 20, 1977. It was the beginning of a remarkable tour of the outer planets. *Voyager 2* was supposed to visit only two planets: Jupiter and Saturn. But back on Earth, space engineers figured out a new flight path; and twelve years and more than 2.8 billion miles after leaving Earth, *Voyager 2* whizzed past the blue storm clouds of Neptune on August 25, 1989. The spacecraft dipped over the north pole of Neptune, raced past its largest moon, Triton, and headed on its way out of the Solar System.

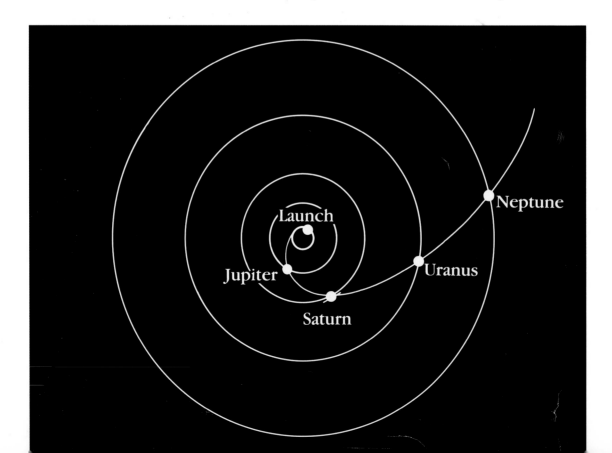

Scientists learned more about Neptune in the few days of *Voyager*'s flyby than in nearly 150 years of observing from Earth. Neptune is so far from us that little was known of the planet except that it was a gas giant with two moons and several "ring arcs," or incomplete rings. Now we have so much information that scientists will need years to examine and understand it all.

Neptune is a turbulent world, with raging winds, giant dark hurricanes, and streaky white clouds of methane-ice that lie thirty-five miles above the lower cloud deck. The inner two-thirds of the planet is a mixture of molten rock, water, liquid ammonia, and methane. The outer third is a heated gas mixture of hydrogen, helium, ammonia, water, and a small amount of methane. Methane in the atmosphere absorbs red light, which is the reason for Neptune's blue color. Haze high above the clouds results in the red rim in this photograph.

Neptune rotates eastward once every sixteen hours and three minutes. Strong frigid winds blow westward in the atmosphere against the planet's rotation at the fastest speeds ever measured on a planet, up to seven hundred miles per hour.

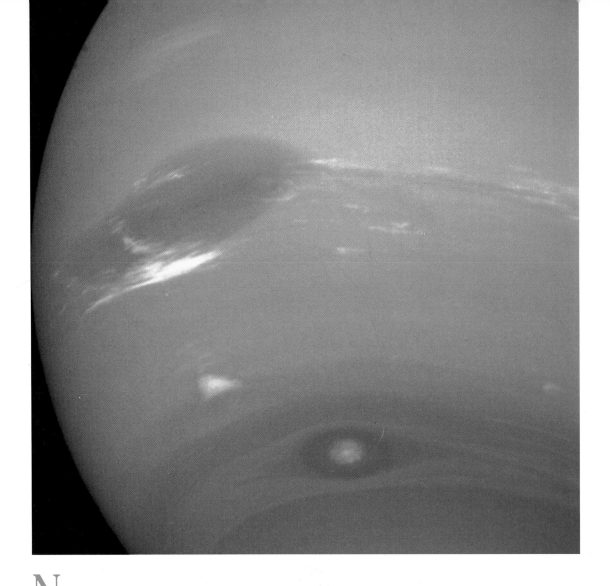

Neptune has two dark storm spots that resemble Jupiter's Great Red Spot. The larger of the two was therefore named the Great Dark Spot. It is a huge tropical storm big enough to swallow our entire planet Earth. South of the Great Dark Spot is a bright white cloud scientists have nicknamed "Scooter." Farther south is the smaller Dark Spot 2.

A close-up view of the Great Dark Spot shows darker and lighter blue areas and streamers of white clouds that change in appearance every few hours. The clouds consist of crystals of methane-ice, unlike the water-ice cirrus clouds found in Earth's atmosphere.

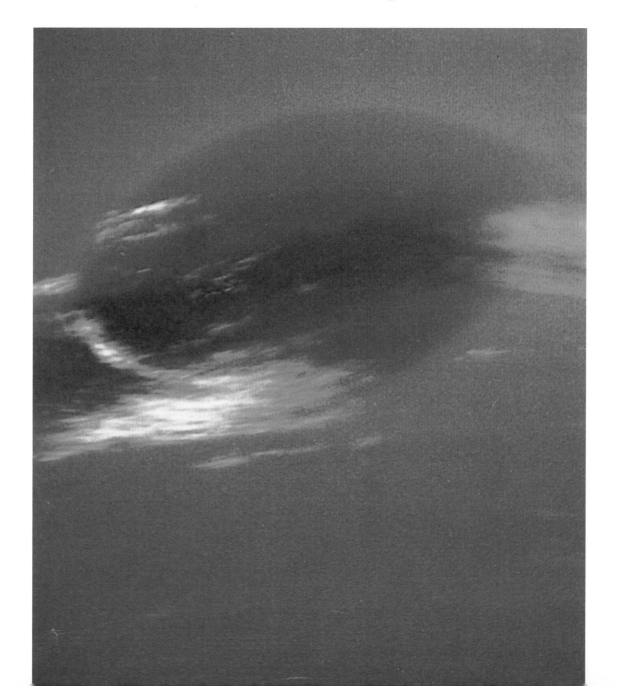

This photo of Neptune shows bands of sunlit cirrus-like clouds in Neptune's northern hemisphere. These clouds cast dark shadows on the blue cloud deck thirty-five miles below. The white streaky clouds are from thirty to over one hundred miles wide and extend for thousands of miles. Scientists cannot yet explain how these clouds form so high in the atmosphere or why they are found in only one location on the planet.

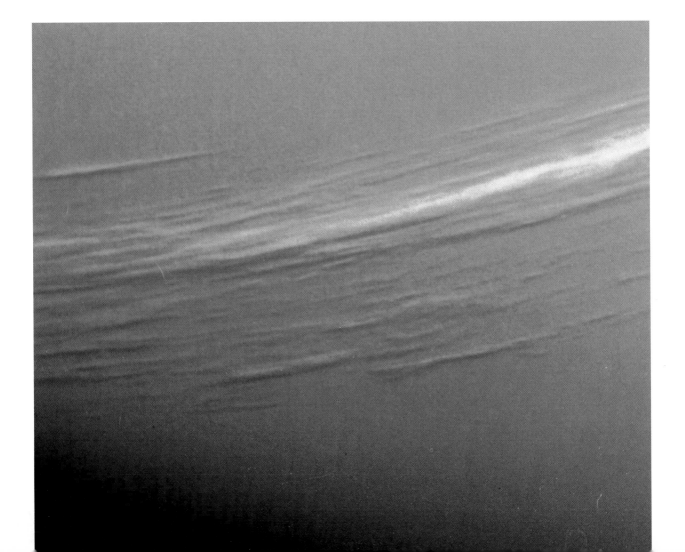

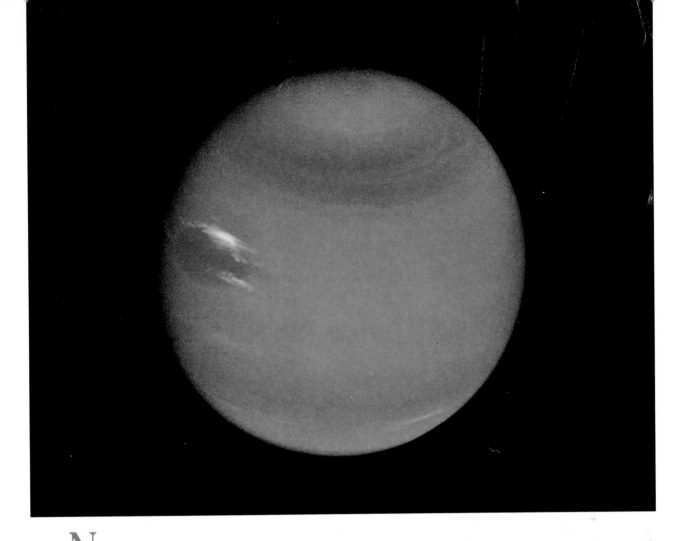

Neptune has some other features that surprised scientists. Neptune's magnetic north and south poles, like those of its neighbor Uranus, are fifty degrees away from its geographic poles. (In contrast, Earth's magnetic and geographic poles are only ten degrees apart.) Another similarity between Neptune and Uranus is that the temperature of the planets' poles and equator is nearly the same, and both are warmer than the midlatitudes.

Like Jupiter, Saturn, and Uranus, Neptune is encircled by a set of rings, and, like the ones around Uranus, Neptune's rings are narrow and very faint.

Neptune has four rings altogether. There are two bright rings, a fainter inner ring, and a sheet of dusty material that may reach down to the planet's cloud tops. The rings are made up of countless tiny particles of dark dust revolving around the planet. This dust is thought to have been caused by tiny meteorites smashing into Neptune's moons over millions of years. The "ring arcs" turned out to be bright clumps in Neptune's complete outer ring. Scientists still are not sure how the clumps in the ring formed.

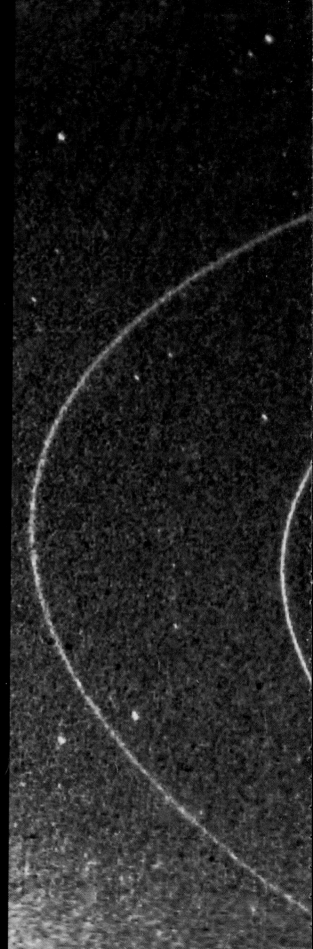

The complete ring system can be seen in this pair of images sent by *Voyager 2*. The planet itself was left out, which is the reason for the black strip in the middle.

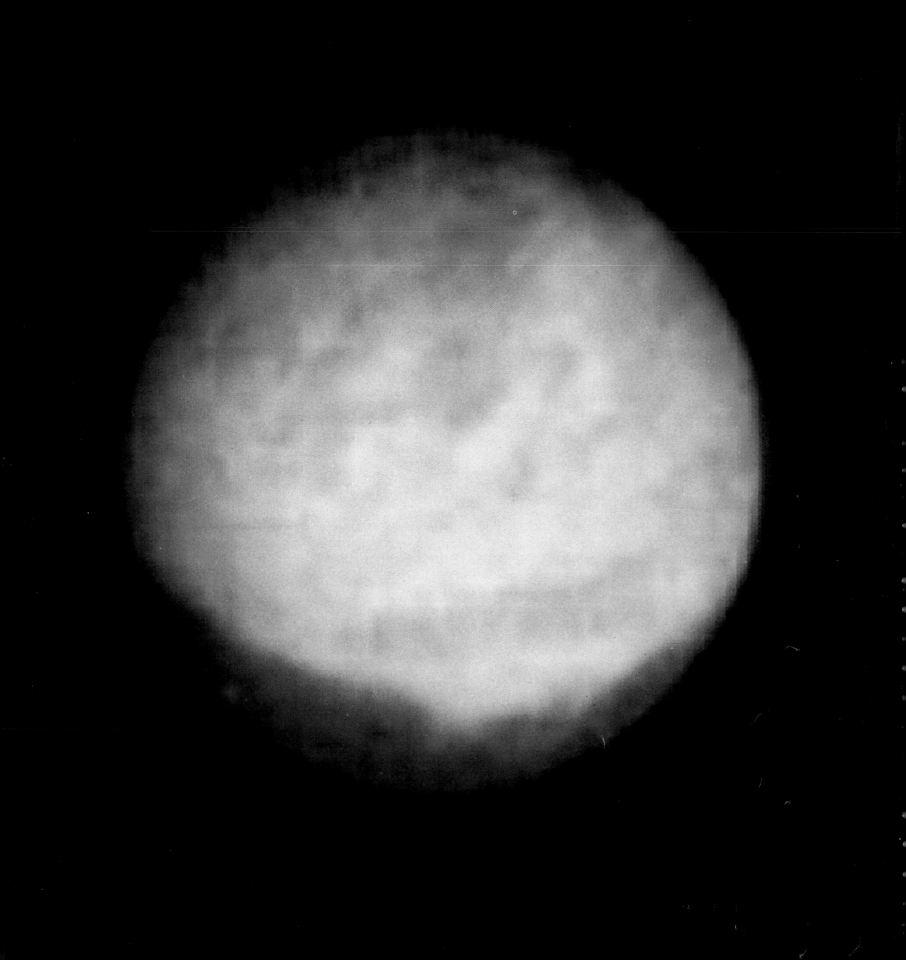

Before *Voyager 2,* scientists thought Neptune had only two moons: Triton and Nereid. Nereid is a small moon, only a few hundred miles across. This moon did not condense from the same matter as Neptune; instead, Nereid resembles a distant asteroid called Chiron. Perhaps Nereid wandered into Neptune's gravitational field and was captured to become a moon.

Triton is much bigger, about 1,700 miles across, nearly as big as our own moon. Also, Triton is the only large moon in the Solar System to orbit in a direction opposite to the planet's rotation. This view of Triton was taken from more than three million miles away by the approaching *Voyager 2* spaceship. It looked like a pinkish ball covered by dark splotches. But Triton turned out to be full of surprises.

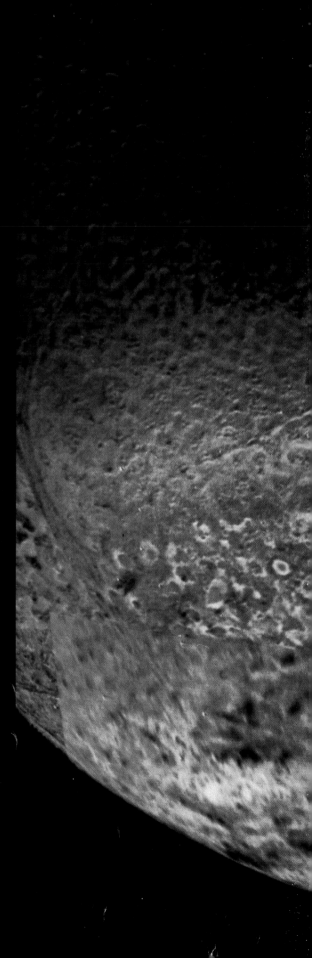

A world unlike any other" is how space scientists described the moon Triton. Triton is colder than any other object ever measured in the Solar System. Even so, its tilted axis and angled orbit give it colder and warmer seasons.

The large south polar cap at the bottom of the photo, now at the height of a forty-one-year-long summer, is a slowly evaporating crust of nitrogen and methane-ice left over from the previous winter. Enormous cracks scar the moon's face. From the ragged edge of the polar cap northward, the surface is white, then darker and redder. Scientists think the red color may be caused by ultraviolet light and other radiation acting on methane gas and ice.

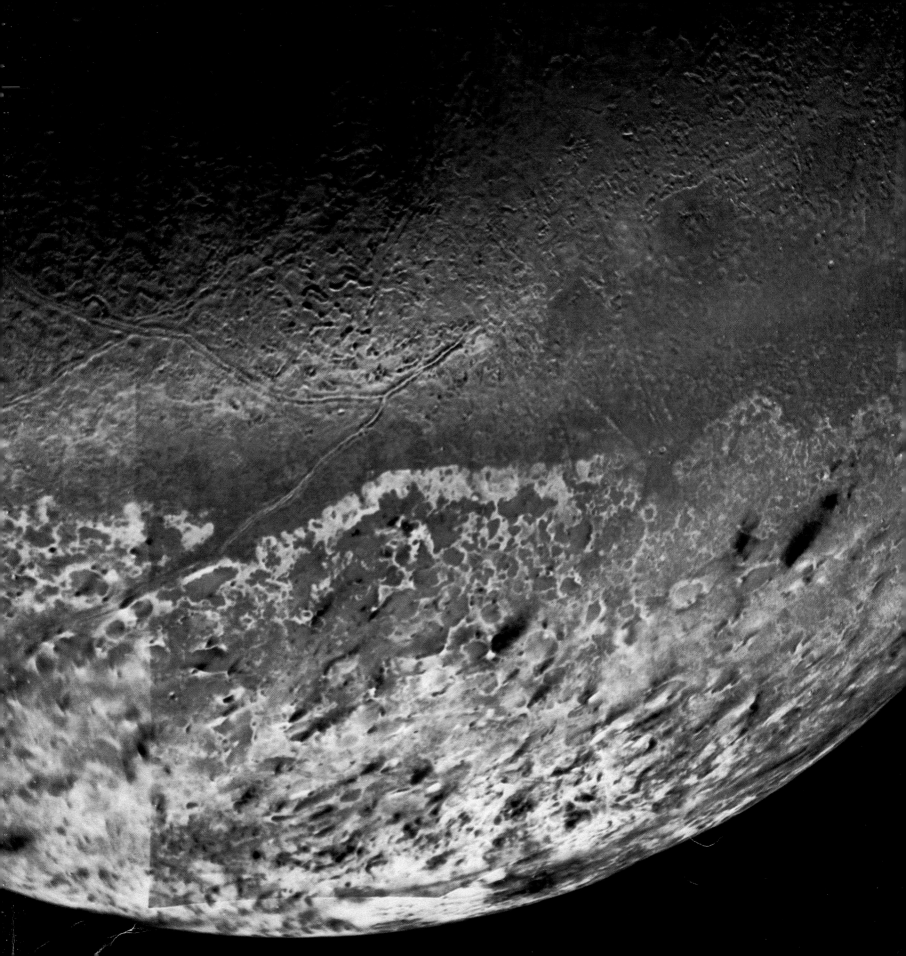

This photo of Triton's surface shows frozen lakes edged by higher terraces. Scientists think that the land has been resurfaced by erupting geysers or volcanoes gushing slushy ice squeezed out of the inside of the moon. When the slush froze solid, it left a smoother surface on the moon. Water-ice is as stiff as rock at the cold temperatures found on Triton.

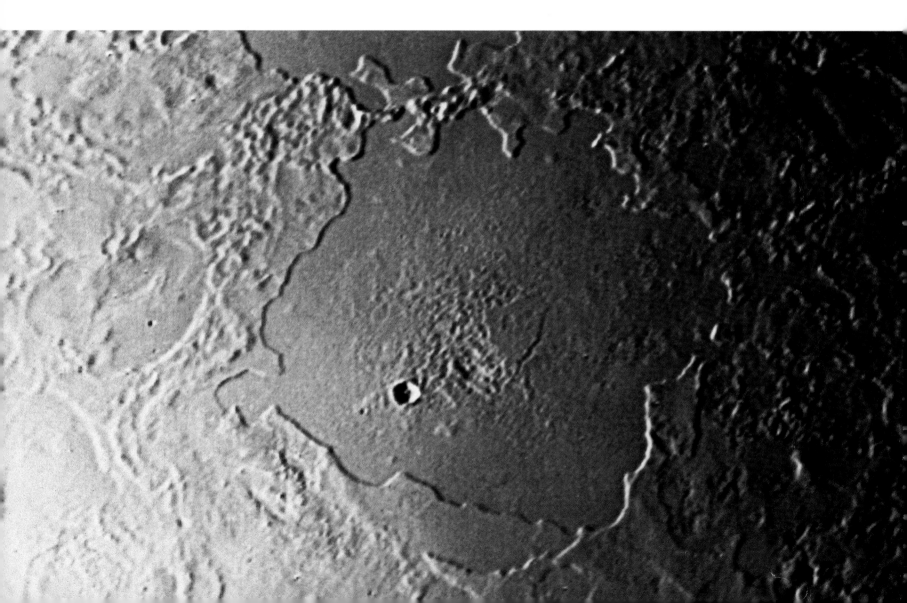

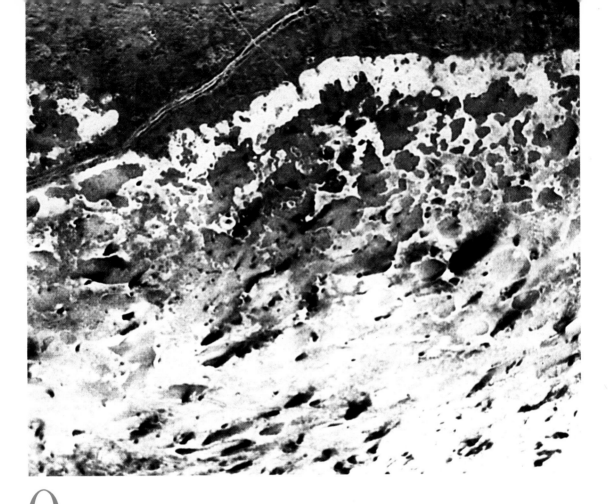

One of the many puzzling things about Triton is the cause of the dark streaks on the south polar cap. Some space scientists suggest that the streaks were made by geyser-like eruptions of nitrogen. Frozen nitrogen might have been heated underground and burst out of the ground, carrying darker materials from the crust upward in giant plumes of dust and gas. The dust would have settled downwind and become visible on the frosty surface of the moon.

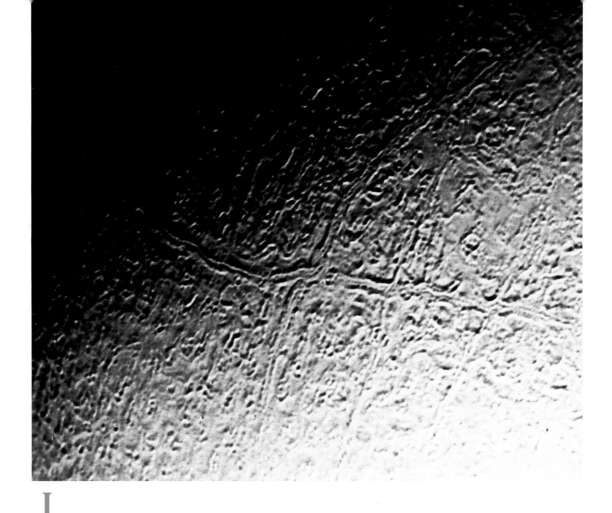

Just above the south polar cap, large parts of Triton's surface look like the rind of a cantaloupe or an orange. This dimpled landscape may have been formed by repeated melting and then hardening over the years. Gigantic cracks, or fault lines, slash across the surface, meeting in huge X's and Y's. Slushy water-ice and ammonia-ice appear to have forced their way upward into some of the cracks, forming central ridges and sometimes overflowing onto the surrounding land.

The signs of past volcanic activity on Triton's surface prove that it was a hotter place a long time ago. Triton may have once been a planet somewhat like Pluto, circling the sun on its own billions of years in the past. Later, Triton was captured by Neptune's gravitational pull and became a moon. One space scientist called Triton "the frozen imprint of that earlier era."

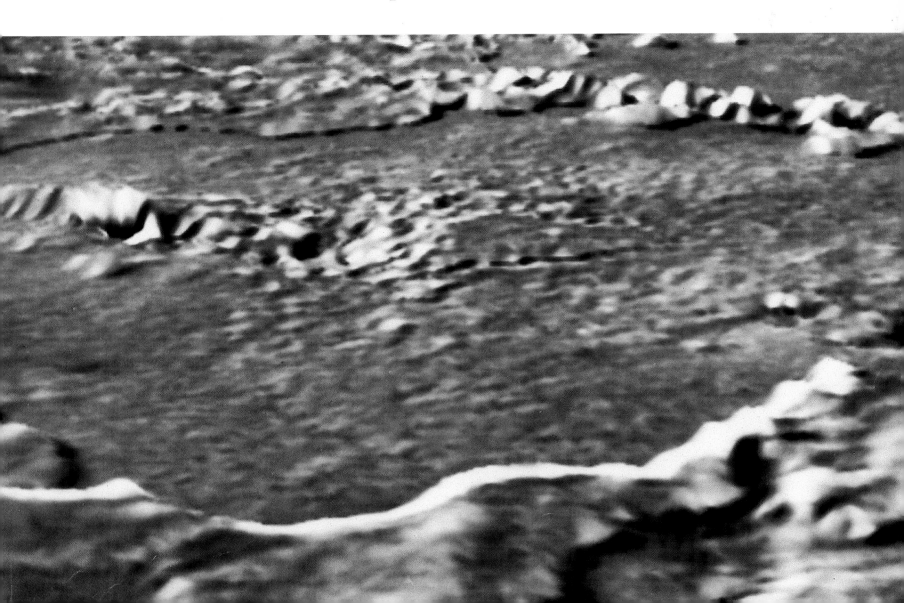

Voyager 2 found six more moons circling Neptune. They were temporarily named 1989N1 through 1989N6. Sometime in the future all the moons will be given real names, probably from mythology. The photo shows satellite 1989N1. It is about 240 miles across and orbits close to the planet. All the moons are dark, irregular-shaped chunks of rock that range from 30 to about 240 miles across. Their meteor-scarred surfaces show that the moons have not been melted since the time they were formed, billions of years ago.

Three days after its flyby, *Voyager 2* took this picture of Neptune and its moon Triton (top). The spaceship's power source should last until about 2015. By then, *Voyager* will reach the heliopause, the true end of the Solar System, where particles from the sun meet interstellar space. Then *Voyager* will drift silently through time and space, a testament to the human search for knowledge.